CONTENTS

KU-412-274

Secrets of the Deep 4

The Right Equipment 6

Feeding Frenzy 8

Reef Life 10

Shipwreck! 12

Eel Encounter 14

Twilight Zone 16

Battle of the Giants 18

Deep Sea Survivors 20

Shock in the Ocean 22

Living in the Depths 24

Over the Edge 26

Deep Sea Discovery 28

Glossary 30

Further Information 31

Index 32

SECRETS OF THE DEEP

Deep beneath the blue surface of the oceans lies an inky-black world. Some of the most fascinating creatures on Earth have been found in these dark, icy waters. Many more may swim there, as yet undiscovered. Our mission is to journey to these depths to find them – are you ready for the trip of a lifetime?

Bottlenose dolphins swim in groups near the ocean surface.

Underwater mountains

Scientists have found out that the ocean floor is smooth and flat in some areas, but covered in underwater mountains in others. Some of these mountains are thousands of metres high but do not even stick out of the water!

Weird and wonderful creatures such as this hatchet fish live in the deep waters of the world's oceans.

THE RIGHT EQUIPMENT

If we had tried to dive to the ocean's depth in our wetsuits, the **pressure** would have crushed our lungs! Instead, we travelled in a **submersible** – a diving machine designed for the deep sea.

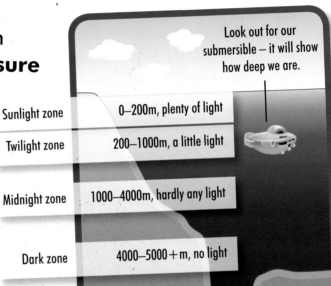

Look out for our submersible – it will show how deep we are.

Sunlight zone	0–200m, plenty of light
Twilight zone	200–1000m, a little light
Midnight zone	1000–4000m, hardly any light
Dark zone	4000–5000+m, no light

trench

OUR SCUBA KIT

- Wetsuit protects diver from cold water, but not from deep sea pressure.
- Air tank provides oxygen for a few hours, but not long enough to travel to deep sea.
- Flippers to help diver swim further, but not for hundreds of metres.

The deeper underwater you go, the greater pressure there is. **SCUBA** divers can only dive safely to about 50 metres.

Our submersible
- Thick steel walls to withstand the high pressures of the deep sea.
- Tough but thin crystal window instead of thick glass.
- Big compressed air tanks: 30 litres (6½ gallons) per person per minute, plus more in case of emergency.
- Propellers to move us in different directions underwater.
- Lights and cameras
- Grab arms to pick up deep sea samples.

A submersible looks a little like an armoured spacecraft!

FEEDING FRENZY

We sank beneath the ocean's surface in our submersible. Straight away we saw a turtle slowly swimming by and then a large, shimmering shoal of small fish.

Predators and prey

The fish had been eating **plankton**, which are tiny floating plants and animals. They were now being attacked. Seabirds dived into the water to peck at the fish. Large tuna fish, dolphins, sealions, and even a humpback whale swam into the shoal to catch their **prey**. This was an ocean feeding frenzy!

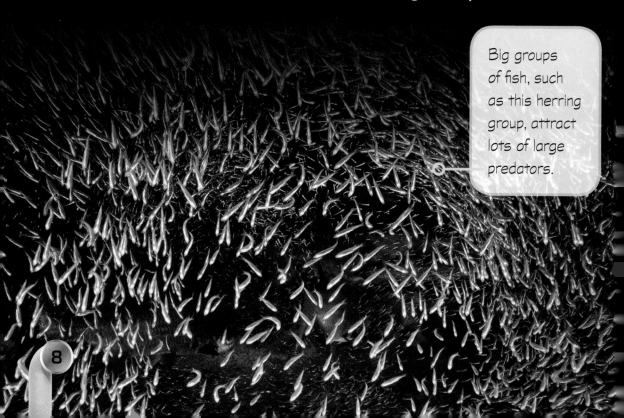

Big groups of fish, such as this herring group, attract lots of large predators.

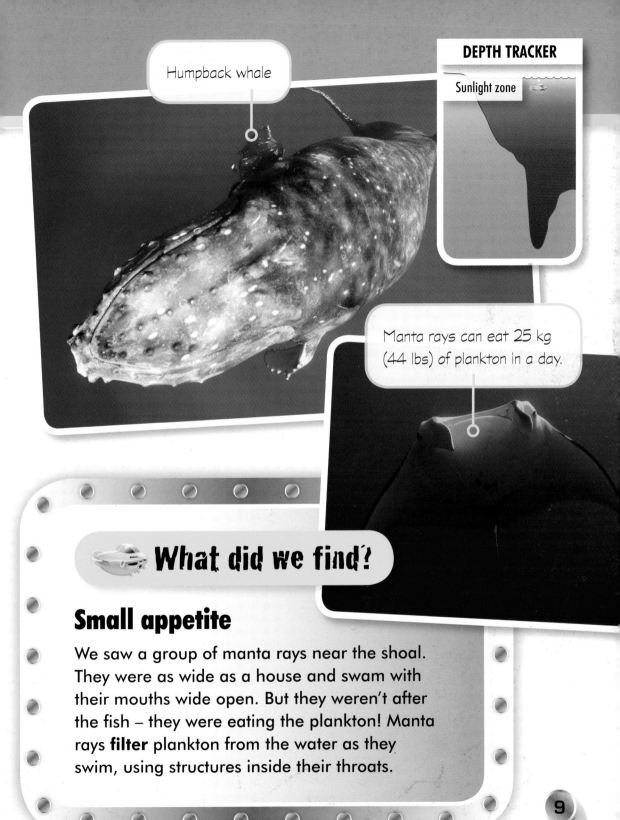

Humpback whale

Manta rays can eat 25 kg (44 lbs) of plankton in a day.

What did we find?

Small appetite

We saw a group of manta rays near the shoal. They were as wide as a house and swam with their mouths wide open. But they weren't after the fish – they were eating the plankton! Manta rays **filter** plankton from the water as they swim, using structures inside their throats.

REEF LIFE

An hour later a reef shark surprised us while we were swimming outside the submerisble to look at a **coral reef** in shallow water. The shark swam close enough for us to look into its black eyes and check out its sharp teeth.

Underwater community

The reef is home to an underwater community. We saw starfish feeding on the coral and colourful fish nibbling on seaweeds. One section of reef appeared to move and I then realized it was not part of the reef, but an octopus instead!

An octopus can change its skin colour to match the area that it is hiding on.

Reef shark

DEPTH TRACKER

Sunlight zone

Corals grow in many different shapes and colours.

What did we find?

Coral reef

Reefs can look like strange rocky plants, but they are made by animals called coral polyps. They build hard coral shelters around their bodies in light, warm seawater. The coral builds up over many years to create reefs. Reefs look tough but they are fragile and easily damaged. We were very careful as we swam back to the submersible.

SHIPWRECK!

As we dropped towards the seafloor we saw the wreck of a ship. At the front there was a jagged hole. We guessed that the ship may have sunk because it hit the reef.

Scallop

 What did we find?

Seafloor life

A spider crab was crawling along the seafloor near the shipwreck, balancing on its long legs. The mud of the seafloor is full of life, which is tasty food for some creatures. Sure enough, the spider crab found some scallops. They looked like swimming false teeth as they tried to escape!

DEPTH TRACKER

Sunlight zone

There are about 3 million shipwrecks in oceans around the world.

Frozen in time

We peered inside the ship through the windows – it was like it had been frozen in time. One cabin had a picture on the wall, half covered by a starfish. In another room we saw broken crockery, tins of food, and a stove, all with yellow **sponges** clinging to them

The *Titanic* is one of the most famous of all shipwrecks.

13

EEL ENCOUNTER

As we swam past the hole in the shipwreck, a pointed face poked out, with its mouth wide open. It was an eel. We watched as its long, spotted body turned and swam back into the gloom of the ship.

Safe inside

Shoals of big, bullet-shaped barracuda fish were hunting for food outside the wreck. We saw that other fish stayed inside. Shipwrecks are a bit like artificial reefs. There are lots of hiding places for animals to keep out of the way of **predators**. Seahorses slowly moved amongst the corals, sponges and weeds that grew on the ship.

Barracudas are fast-swimming fish with razor-sharp teeth.

Moray eels often rest with their mouths open. This helps them to breathe.

What did we find?

Poisonous lion

The lion fish is only about 30 cm (12 in) long but it came right up to the submersible. It is a beautiful striped fish with lots of long, pointed spines. It was unafraid because its spines are weapons. If one jabbed you it would really hurt and make you very ill.

TWILIGHT ZONE

We pressed our faces to the glass of a side window and looked into the dark. We could see the flashing lights of cuttlefish and jellyfish. The rounded top of one jellyfish must have been 2 metres (about 6 ft) across. Thank goodness we were inside the submersible and out of reach of all those stinging tentacles.

Jellyfish

Cuttlefish send messages to each other by flashing light in the dark.

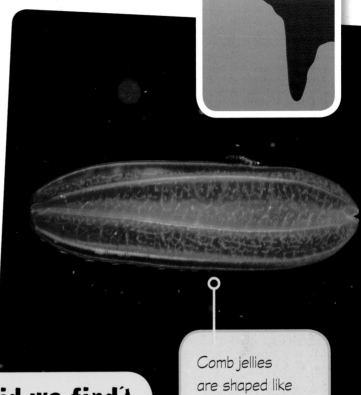

Twilight zone

Deeper and darker

We had reached the twilight zone of the ocean about half a kilometre (¼ mile) down. Only a tiny amount of sunlight can reach these depths. Outside the temperature was dropping and the pressure was rising as we went deeper.

 What did we find?

Comb jellies are shaped like gooseberries and glow in the dark.

Lighting up the deep

Many deep sea animals produce their own light. Chemicals in their bodies mix and react to release light, rather like glow sticks. The animals make light for different reasons. Some use light to find their way in the dark, others to attract mates or to draw prey closer so they can eat them.

BATTLE OF THE GIANTS

At 800 metres (2,600 ft) deep there was a huge whack on the side of the submersible. We rushed to look through the window and saw a giant squid! Its **tentacles** were trying to grip on to the submersible. This animal must have been 10 metres (32 ft) long.

Squid hunter!

Just then, an even bigger shape appeared fast out of the darkness. It was a sperm whale and it was hunting the squid. The squid tried to get away but the whale grabbed it firmly.

Sperm whales can stay underwater for more than two hours.

What did we find?

Swimming deep

Whales need to breathe air to survive. A whale takes many huge gulps of air before it dives. It stores most of the oxygen from the air in its muscles and blood.

SQUID EYES

A giant squid's eyes can be as big as a soccer ball! They are like headlights to help the squid see in the dark.

We eventually reached deep, black water. We came across an angler fish. The tip of the antennae above its mouth looked like a wiggling piece of tasty food. The angler fish was also lit up. It was ready to snap up any fish attracted by this clever trick.

Adapted for eating

There is not much food for animals down here, so predators need special features to help them survive in the dark. The angler fish has its light. The deep sea gulper has wide jaws. It can fit a much larger animal than itself in its mouth.

Most angler fish are only the size of a person's fist.

Midnight zone

Sea cucumbers chew up any bits of dead animals that fall to the ocean floor.

What did we find?

Deep sea suckers

We saw strange marks, a bit like tyre tracks, across the ocean floor. We realized that sea cucumbers were leaving tracks as they slowly moved along. Sea cucumbers suck up mud on the ocean floor into their stomachs, to extract any hidden bits of food that might be in the mud.

SHOCK IN THE OCEAN

Without any warning the submersible suddenly lurched to the side, and was out of control. It tumbled against a rock and the lights went off for a moment. It must have been an underwater earthquake.

The deep sea is completely dark. Only artificial lights can show what is down there.

An underwater earthquake can create an enormous wave, called a tsunami.

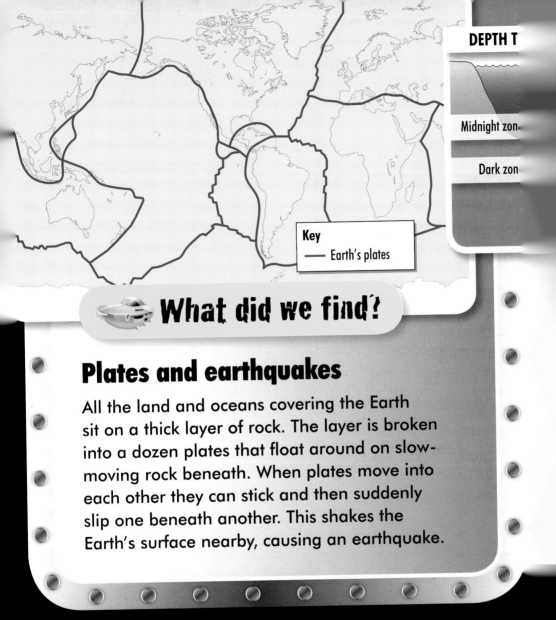

Key
— Earth's plates

What did we find?

Plates and earthquakes

All the land and oceans covering the Earth sit on a thick layer of rock. The layer is broken into a dozen plates that float around on slow-moving rock beneath. When plates move into each other they can stick and then suddenly slip one beneath another. This shakes the Earth's surface nearby, causing an earthquake.

Growing rock

We just saw some rock growing! We were at a place where plates were pulling apart. This left a crack through which liquid rock was seeping from inside the Earth. It soon cooled down in the cold seawater and set hard. So this is how underwater mountains can grow

LIVING IN THE DEPTHS

Out of the window we saw pale **crabs**, **mussels**, and long red **tubeworms** clustered around what looked like a chimney with black smoke coming out of it. This was a **hydrothermal vent**.

Extreme food web

The vent was hot and full of bits of dissolved rocks called **minerals**. Tiny living things called **bacteria** thrive there. They make food from the minerals. Mussels filter the bacteria from the water, then eat them. Crabs and other creatures feed on the mussels.

Red tubeworms live near hydrothermal vents. They can grow to be taller than a man!

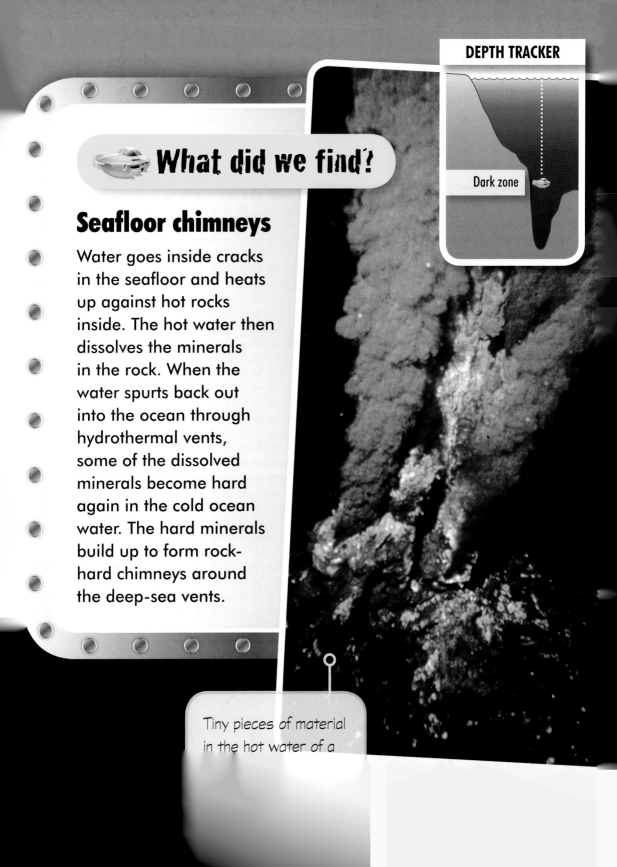

Dark zone

What did we find?

Seafloor chimneys

Water goes inside cracks in the seafloor and heats up against hot rocks inside. The hot water then dissolves the minerals in the rock. When the water spurts back out into the ocean through hydrothermal vents, some of the dissolved minerals become hard again in the cold ocean water. The hard minerals build up to form rock-hard chimneys around the deep-sea vents.

Tiny pieces of material in the hot water of a

OVER THE EDGE

Suddenly the seafloor in front of us just disappeared. We had reached the edge of an ocean trench. Trenches are dips in the seafloor caused by one plate moving underneath another one. They are the deepest places on Earth.

Reaching the limit

We dropped over the edge and fell fast. Soon we were 7,000 metres (23,000 ft) deep. The water pressure here was 700 times greater than at the ocean surface. The lights shone on some giant isopods – crab-like creatures that live in deep water.

This submarine has reached the bottom of a deep sea trench.

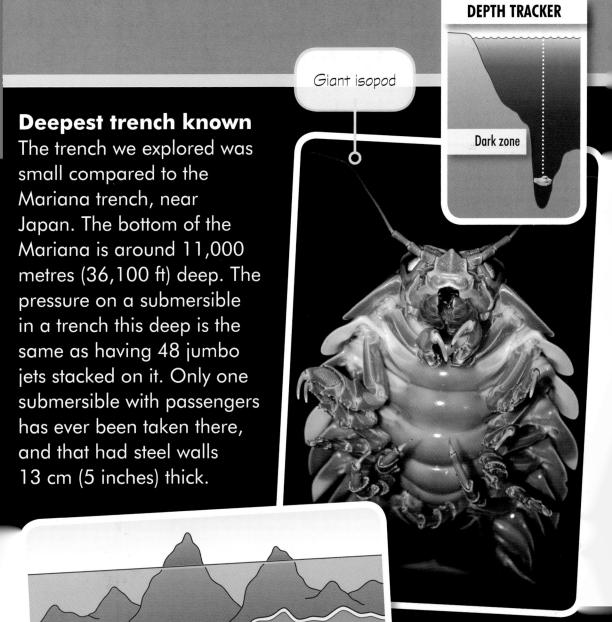

Giant isopod

Dark zone

Deepest trench known

The trench we explored was small compared to the Mariana trench, near Japan. The bottom of the Mariana is around 11,000 metres (36,100 ft) deep. The pressure on a submersible in a trench this deep is the same as having 48 jumbo jets stacked on it. Only one submersible with passengers has ever been taken there, and that had steel walls 13 cm (5 inches) thick.

The Mariana trench was formed when two plates pushed together to create a deep cut in the seabed.

DEEP SEA DISCOVERY

Last night we finally returned to the surface. We took with us some of the bacteria we found in the sea vents. This may help scientists to find out more about other, harmful bacterias.

Ocean around us

As we surfaced we saw fishing boats pulling along a giant net. People are catching so many fish that there are not many left of some species. Trawler nets can damage reefs and harm sea life. Scientists and fishing crews must work together to care for the oceans.

Huge amounts of fish and other sea creatures are caught in fishing boat nets.

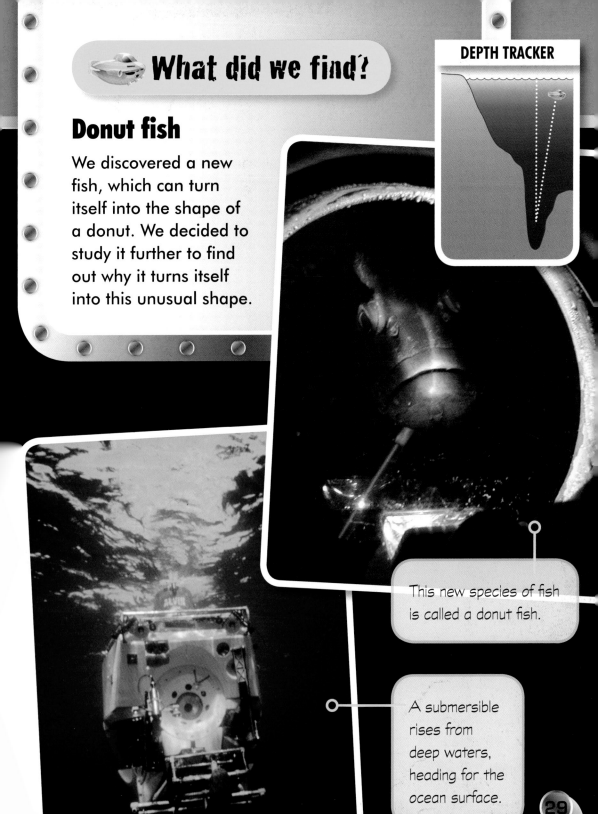

What did we find?

Donut fish

We discovered a new fish, which can turn itself into the shape of a donut. We decided to study it further to find out why it turns itself into this unusual shape.

This new species of fish is called a donut fish.

A submersible rises from deep waters, heading for the ocean surface.

29

GLOSSARY

bacteria very simple microscopic living things

coral reef underwater feature mainly found in warm seas, made of the skeletons of coral animals

crab type of ten-legged animal with a tough shell, claws, and eyes on short stalks, usually found on shores or the seafloor

filter to pass liquid through a fine barrier so that it is let through, but solid pieces are trapped in the barrier

hydrothermal vent an opening in Earth's crust, deep beneath the ocean surface

mineral natural substance that makes up rocks

mussel type of animal with two hinged, long shells, mostly found on the seafloor and rocks

plankton mixture of tiny plants and animals that drift or float through the oceans

predator animal that hunts and eats other animals, such as a shark

pressure force pressing against something, such as the force of water on someone diving

prey animal that is eaten by other animals, such as a herring

SCUBA short for 'self contained underwater breathing apparatus'

sponge marine animals that live together in a blob-like shape with holes over the surface through which they take in food

submersible vessel that can dive, often taking people, deep underwater

tentacle long organ near the mouth of animals including octopus and anemones, which they use to feel, feed, or grasp

tubeworm type of marine worm that lives in a hard tube it makes

FURTHER INFORMATION

Websites

Find out more about deep sea life at:

www.teachers.ash.org.au/jmresources/deep/creatures.html or **http://deepsealife.net/**

People have used all sorts of submersibles to explore the oceans. To learn more, visit:

www.pbs.org/wgbh/nova/abyss/frontier/deepsea.html

Would you like to know more about the world's oceans, the life they hold, and the problems they face? One place to start is:

www.panda.org/about_our_earth/blue_planet/

Books

Monsters of the Deep: Deep Sea Adaptation by Kelly Regan Barnhill. Fact Finders (2008).

Extreme Science: Life in the Crusher by Trevor Day. A & C Black (2009).

Underwater Exploration (Restless Sea) by Carole Garbuny Vogel. Children's Press (2003).

DVD

Blue Planet, narrated by David Attenborough (BBC, 2005)

INDEX

air 6, 7, 19
angler fish 20

bacteria 24, 28
barracuda 14
bottlenose dolphins 4

coral reef 10–11
corals 10–11, 14
cuttlefish 16

dark zone 22–27
divers 6
donut fish 29

earthquakes 22–23
eels 14–15

hatchet fish 5
hydrothermal vents 24–25, 28

isopods 26

jellyfish 16, 17

lights 16, 17, 20, 22
lion fish 15

manta rays 9
midnight zone 19–23
minerals 24–25
mountains 5, 23

ocean floor 5
octopus 10
oxygen 6, 19

plankton 8, 9
plates 23
poisonous 15
polyps 11
predators 14
pressure 6, 7, 26

reef shark 10, 11

scallops 12
scuba divers 6
sea cucumber 21
seafloor chimneys 25
shipwrecks 12–15
shoal 8
sponges 13
squid 18–19
submersibles 6–7, 27, 29
sunlight zone 6, 8–15

tsunami 22
trenches 26–27
tubeworms 24
twilight zone 16–19

whales 8, 9, 18–19

zones under the sea 6